Cowboy and a Pig That's Not Too Big

Diane Odegard Gockel

ISBN: 0989631753
ISBN 13: 9780989631754

Dedication

To our oldest son, Dan, who models the highest of character and values. I just love and admire your enthusiasm for life! We love you. And to our neighbors and visitors who bring Cowboy and his pasture mates carrots and treats daily. Our rescues so look forward to your visits. Lastly, to Cowboy: your big personality is a big hit on the farm!

About the Author:

Diane Odegard Gockel is a former high-school teacher who has devoted much of her life to the rescue, fostering, and adoption of homeless pets. She and her daughter, Julie Diane Stafford, co-own Unplug and Create. Diane and her husband have four grown children and live on a small farm in Sammamish, Washington, called Second Chance Ranch.

Other books in the Rescue Series by

Diane Odegard Gockel

The Rescue of Winks

Bella Saves the Farm

Al the Alpaca: Forever Friends

Fancy Has a Plan

Pat and the Gabby Goats

Cowboy and a Pig That's Not Too Big

The Farm Lady named me Cowboy on the day that I came to the farm. Like all the animals on Second Chance Ranch that live with the Farm Family, I was rescued and adopted. I am a Jersey steer, and I am very big. I weigh about two thousand pounds! I love living on this farm, but it took a little getting used to. Actually, it took the other animals a little getting used to me!

I was not born here on Second Chance Ranch. I was born on another small cattle farm and bottle-fed by the farmer's daughter. She really liked me and wanted to make sure that I lived a long and safe life. As I grew up and got much bigger, it was harder and harder for her to keep me. Because I was too big, the farmer's daughter began to search for a new home for me, but it seemed no one wanted a big steer as a pet. That's when the Farm Lady heard about me and agreed to adopt me.

I arrived at her farm in a very big trailer. When the trailer doors opened, I saw the Farm Lady for the first time. She could tell that I was scared and very unhappy about going for a ride in a trailer. But she had carrots in her hands, and carrots happen to be a favorite food of mine, so I inched my way out of the trailer toward her. My hooves stood in the rich green grass that was now my pasture. As I looked around, I spotted a white horse nearby, looking right at me. I was just thinking how glad I was to have a pasture mate when suddenly the white horse turned and ran away!

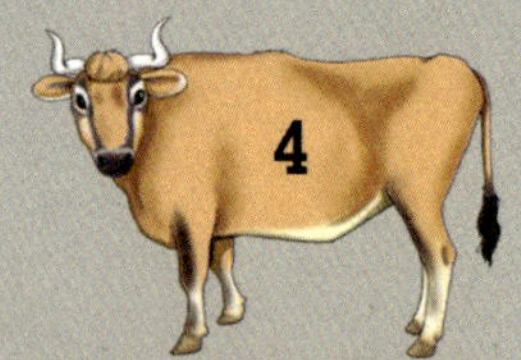

"Don't worry about silly Cruiser the horse. He's just a bit afraid of you because you're so big," explained the Farm Lady. "Soon you will be the best of friends." I felt sad that Cruiser was so afraid of me. I really was looking forward to making friends. As I looked around, though, I could see lots of other animals as well: goats, alpacas, donkeys, two miniature horses, and a llama. I was so excited to meet them all!

After the Farm Lady left, I began to enjoy the sweet taste of the rich green grass. I had only been given hay at my last farm, and this grass tasted so much better. As I was grazing, I spotted a few goats resting under an old apple tree. I decided to head on over and introduce myself.

"Hello, goats! My name is Cowboy, and I am new here. I thought I would come over and meet you all."

The goats, clearly startled, looked up at me. I could see the fear in their eyes as they suddenly took off running toward their barn. My head dropped, and I was overwhelmed with sadness. How will I ever make friends if everybody is afraid of me? I thought.

As night approached, I slowly headed over to the big barn, hoping to get a good night's sleep. Perhaps I would have better luck making friends tomorrow. But for tonight, I felt sad and lonely. I found it difficult to get my big horns through the stall door but managed to find my way through to the hay trough. The hay was heaped up green and soft, but I was too lonely to eat.

"Hey, big guy, do you happen to see where my apple went?" Surprised to find I was not alone and somebody was actually talking to me, I leaned my head over the half-wall to the neighboring stall to find a small pink pig looking right up at me!

"Are you talking to me, little pig?" I wondered out loud.

"Of course, big guy," affirmed the pig. "The Farm Lady likes to hide apples and peanuts in my hay bed, and I seem to have misplaced one apple. I thought, since you are so tall, you could see it from up there."

After scanning the pig's very clean stall, sure enough, I spotted the apple.

"It's closer to your water bucket. Just a little bit farther that way," I said, pointing with my horns. "Aren't you afraid to talk to me too?" I added.

"Nope," the pig said as he headed toward the water bucket to retrieve his prized apple. "You seem nice enough to me."

"No one else would talk with me today. They all ran away. They are afraid of me because I am just too big," I explained in a voice that could not hide my sadness. "I am afraid I will never have a friend."

"First," said the pig as he munched away at his apple, "you are not too big. You are just the right size for a steer. And secondly, I will be your friend. So there, you have one friend. Now, if you wouldn't mind helping me find the peanuts. They're in here somewhere..." I felt my spirit beginning to lift as I watched the pig root his nose through the pile of hay, sniffing for peanuts.

That evening, I made my first friend—Bentley the pig. I helped him find peanuts, and we chatted until we both dozed off for the night. The next day, I attempted to make more friends, but each time the farm animals avoided me. My size clearly scared them. When I entered my stall that following evening, I was grateful to see my friend, Bentley, on the other side of the wall.

"Any luck finding friends today, Cowboy?" questioned Bentley as he lay in his hay pile half asleep.

"No. No luck at all. I'm just too big," I said.

"You are just the size you are meant to be. Not too big at all," Bentley assured me.

In frustration with Bentley, I quipped, "I am so too big. You have no idea what it is like to be too big."

Bentley looked straight up at me through narrowed, serious eyes. "I do too know what it is like to be too big," he said. "That is why I am here. I was thought to be too big once myself."

I could not understand how a little pig could be too big.

Bentley stood up and continued.

"I was purchased as an indoor pet when I was just a small piglet. My first owner was told that I wouldn't get much bigger, but I did. I got a lot bigger! She decided that I was too big for her house, so she gave me away. After being moved from place to place, I was lucky enough to be adopted by the Farm Lady. Now that I live outside, I realize that I am not too big at all. I was just in the wrong place. I am exactly the size I am supposed to be, and so are you, Cowboy. Eventually, the other rescues on the farm will see you and not your size. Give them time. Now, help me find that peach. I can sniff it. I know it's here somewhere."

That night, I thought a lot about Bentley's story. It must have been hard for him to feel too big. The next morning, still thinking about Bentley, I headed out to the apple tree to shade myself and maybe get a bite to eat. As I approached the tree, I noticed the older white goat resting underneath it. Feeling encouraged by Bentley's story, I approached him. As I did, my horns accidently bumped the tree branch, and an apple dropped right on top of the old goat's head! Oh no, I thought.

"I am so sorry, Mr. Goat! I did not mean to drop an apple on your head! I guess I am just too big, and my horns hit the branches. I hope I didn't hurt you," I explained.

The goat stood up, shook his head, and to my surprise did not run away.

"Hello, Cowboy. I'm Pat. Nice to finally meet you."

"Oh, it is so great to meet you too, Pat!" I said excitedly. "I thought you might be afraid of me because I am too big."

"Well," Pat said as he munched on the apple that had bounced off his head, "I will say that the other goats heard about you and were concerned about your size. So as their leader, I said I would go check you out. Seems they have never seen a steer before. You seem friendly enough to me. Plus, your size might just come in handy."

"How so?" I questioned.

As Pat backed away from the apple tree, I could see the other goats watching us on the crest of the hill.

"Now, Cowboy," said Pat, "use those big horns and rattle those branches. See if you can make some apples fall."

"Oh, sure!" I said. "I think I just might be big enough."

Stretching my neck as long as I could, I felt my horns touch the branches, and I began to shake the large tree. Suddenly, I felt an apple drop on my back. And then another and another, and soon, the ground was covered with apples!

Pat was delighted as he saw all the apples on the ground.

"C'mon over, goats!" he called to his companions. "Cowboy has prepared a wonderful lunch for us." Seconds later, all the goats were under the tree with me, eating apples. Even Cruiser the horse joined us!

"Thank you, Cowboy!" said Dahlia.

"You're the best!" affirmed Daisy.

"You're not scary or mean at all," added Bailey.

"He's just big," explained Cruiser.

"But not too big," I added as I felt the joy of having friends again.

That afternoon, the goats introduced me to all the other animals on the farm. Al the Alpaca introduced me to Teddy Bear and his friend Francis, who told us wonderful stories. Huck and Logan showed me where to find blackberries, and Cruiser showed me how fast he could run before we took a nap under the apple tree. I was so happy to have so many wonderful friends on the farm.

That night, I couldn't wait to talk to my good friend Bentley.

"How was your day?" Bentley snorted as I walked into my stall.

"I made new friends today, Bentley. They are really nice, and they like me too. They even like how big I am!"

Bentley seemed pleased as he looked up at me.

"They didn't think you were too big?" Bentley said jokingly.

"Of course not, Bentley. I'm not too big. I'm just the size I am meant to be. I'm a steer, you know," I said, playing along.

"Yes, you are," Bentley said affectionately. "Now, big guy, help me find those apples."

As I helped Bentley locate all the treats the Farm Lady hid in his hay pile, I couldn't help but wonder how Bentley knew I would someday be accepted by the other animals on the farm.

As though he heard my thoughts, Bentley said, "Sometimes we are misunderstood, Cowboy. Like, many people think that pigs are messy because we roll in the mud. But pigs don't sweat, so we do it to keep cool. Pigs are actually very tidy. But, we have small eyes and do not see well, so we root in the dirt to find our food. Your friends thought you might be dangerous to them because you are big, but they too were wrong."

"Pigs are also very smart," I added. "And they make good friends."

I watched as Bentley nestled himself under his hay pile and fell asleep. As I looked around his stall, I saw that it was indeed clean and tidy. I, too, had been surprised by a clean pig. I felt grateful that he gave me a chance to be his friend.

The Real Cowboy

The Real Cruiser

The Real Bentley